The Horse Whisperer

NICHOLAS EVANS

Level 3

Retold by Andy Hopkins and Jocelyn Potter
Series Editors: Andy Hopkins and Jocelyn Potter

Pearson Education Limited
Edinburgh Gate, Harlow,
Essex CM20 2JE, England
and Associated Companies throughout the world.

ISBN 0 582 41637X

First published in Great Britain by Transworld Publishers Ltd
This adaptation first published by Addison Wesley Longman Limited
in the Longman Fiction Series 1997
This edition first published 1999

Second impression 2000

Original copyright © Nicholas Evans 1995
This edition copyright © Penguin Books Ltd 1999
Illustrations by David Frankland
Cover design by Bender Richardson White

The right of Nicholas Evans to be identified as author of *The Horse Whisperer* has been
asserted in accordance with the Copyright, Designs and Patents Act 1988

Set in 11/14pt Bembo
Printed in Spain by Mateu Cromo, S. A. Pinto (Madrid)

Published by Pearson Education Limited in association with
Penguin Books Ltd, both companies being subsidiaries of Pearson Plc

For a complete list of the titles available in the Penguin Readers series please write to your local
Pearson Education office or to: Marketing Department, Penguin Longman Publishing,
5 Bentinck Street London W1M 5RN.

Contents

Introduction

Nicholas Evans was born in Bromsgrove, England, in 1950. He studied law at Oxford University, and then he began writing for a newspaper in Newcastle. Later he changed jobs and went to work in television. He became a reporter in the United States and the Middle East and one of his jobs was to write about the war in Beirut. He also produced television programmes about the lives of important people. In 1985 Evans turned from fact to fiction. Since then he has written and produced films for television. He lives in South London with his wife and their two children.

The Horse Whisperer first became famous in 1995, a year before it was completed. The story was sold to Robert Redford and Hollywood Pictures for $3 million. Evans had the idea for the book when a friend told him about a man in Dartmoor, in the south of England. This man could calm a wild horse just by talking quietly to it. Tom Booker, in *The Horse Whisperer*, is a similar kind of man. He wins the trust of horses because he knows and loves them.

The story, though, does not take place in England. Tom Booker lives and works in the wide-open spaces of Montana in the United States. Evans wrote the book in England. But he spent time in Montana, New Mexico and Northern California making notes for it. This gives the book a strong sense of place. Important storylines run through the book. Feelings between a mother and daughter change and grow. The mother has to choose between her work and her family, but she also has to understand her own real needs. It is a story of love and self-discovery. Evans says: 'It's about people finding a way of life that is true to themselves and the world.'

Grace, who is thirteen years old, is the only child of Robert and Annie. Robert is a busy New York lawyer and Annie, an Englishwoman, works on a fashionable magazine. Their lives are changed for ever when Grace and her much-loved horse, Pilgrim, are both badly hurt in a riding accident. Annie wants to help her daughter to get better. She also wants to save the horse's life. In Annie's mind, the lives of her daughter and the horse are tied together in a way that she cannot explain, even to herself. She hears of the special skills that Tom Booker has with horses. At first he says that he is unable to do anything for Pilgrim. But Annie does not accept this. She drives with her daughter and the sick horse all the way to Montana to make him change his mind.

Chapter 1   The Accident

High in the woods that morning, snow covered the ground and ice hung from the trees. There was a silence and calm that you could almost touch; no bird or animal spoke.

Into this silence came two horses, one brown and one black, walking through the deep snow. Their riders, two girls of thirteen and fourteen, were laughing.

The older girl, Judith, was leading the way on Gulliver, the brown horse, and looking back over her shoulder at Pilgrim.

'Look at him, Grace! He's so funny.'

Grace was laughing too much to reply. Her horse was walking with his head down, pushing his nose through the snow. Every now and then he suddenly lifted his head and threw the snow into the air. Then he jumped playfully when it fell.

'That's enough, you!' Grace told him finally.

They made their way slowly down through the woods to an old road that was not often used now. A river ran along the side of it. They were looking for an old railway bridge that passed over the river.

'There it is.' Judith saw the bridge.

The path up from the road was very steep.

Judith went first. Her horse, Gulliver, took a few steps and then stopped.

'Up we go, boy,' Judith told him.

Gulliver felt the ground with his foot and then continued to climb. When her friend was almost at the top, Grace started to follow on Pilgrim.

'How is it?' she called.

'It's not too bad,' replied Judith. 'But go slowly.'

Suddenly Grace heard the sound of Gulliver's shoe hitting ice.

1

He lifted his front legs towards the truck . . .

Judith gave a loud cry. Then Gulliver dropped to his knees and fell back down towards the road.

Grace tried to move Pilgrim out of the way, but there was no time. Gulliver hit Pilgrim hard and both horses and their riders landed in the road. Judith was hanging from the horse by one foot. Then her head hit the hard ice and she stopped moving.

Suddenly a large truck came round the corner. The driver saw the horses in front of him, but it was too late; he couldn't stop quickly enough on the icy road. What were those children doing? Couldn't they hear him? Couldn't they see him?

Grace, holding tightly onto Pilgrim's back, could see the truck. She tried to reach Gulliver and lead him and Judith off the road. She pulled at Pilgrim and turned him towards the other horse. But there was not enough time. The truck was almost on top of them. Then the driver sounded his horn.

Pilgrim seemed to go crazy. He lifted his front legs towards the truck, and Grace was thrown into the road.

For years afterwards the truck driver had a clear memory of that moment. The horse's face was covered in blood, and his eyes were wild. He seemed to throw himself against the front window of the truck. Then the driver saw nothing more through the broken glass. He could not stop the truck. It continued to move across the ice before it finally came to a stop under the bridge.

◆

Grace's father, Robert, got back from the shops and found two messages on the answering machine of his weekend home in Chatham. One was from Annie, his wife, who was working late in New York. The other was from Mrs Dyer, at the stables where they kept Pilgrim. Something in Mrs Dyer's voice made Robert go cold. Soon afterwards he was on the telephone to his wife at her office. Grace was in hospital, he told Annie quietly. She was very badly hurt. Her friend Judith was dead.

On the train from New York, Annie Maclean thought about her life since her daughter's birth. She was proud to be back at work only six weeks after Grace was born. She had a young child, but she also had an important job with a top magazine. It wasn't too bad at first; Annie could sometimes work at home. And she often took Grace with her when she had to work out of town.

But now Annie worked long hours. She and Grace had little time together. In the mornings, Grace had to do her piano practice before school. They also spent two hours together each evening. But Annie made sure that Grace did her homework then. She tried to show her love for her daughter. She knew, though, that she often seemed cold and impatient with her.

They were more relaxed together during their weekends in the country, because they were both interested in horses. Annie didn't ride these days, but she understood the riding world. She liked taking Grace to horse shows. If the girl wanted to talk, though, she always turned to her father first.

◆

Pilgrim was down by the river when they found him. There was dry blood all over his face, and fresh blood was pouring from a large hole in his chest. Even in this state, he was clearly a beautiful animal. But Harry Logan, the horse doctor, did not think that he could live for very long; he was losing too much blood.

Logan walked towards the horse. He spoke to him softly, trying to hide the needle in his hand.

'It's all right, boy. Don't worry. Nobody's going to hurt you.'

The horse took a few sudden steps and fell. Logan ran to him and pushed the needle deep into his neck.

◆

When she arrived at the hospital, Annie noted her husband's pale face and the deep unhappiness in his eyes. She put her arms around him without speaking.

'How is she?' Annie finally asked.

'She's going to be all right,' Robert said. 'She can't move, or talk. But the tests show no signs of brain damage.' He stopped and tried to fight against the tears. Annie waited. She knew that there was more.

'Tell me,' she said.

He looked at the floor and then slowly back at her.

'It's her leg.'

'How bad is it?' she asked.

'It's bad. They're . . . they're taking it off.'

Annie surprised herself. Robert was crying, so she didn't. Someone had to stay calm.

'Which leg is it?'

'The right one.'

'How much of it are they taking off?'

Robert looked at her strangely.

'From above the—' For a moment he could not continue. 'Above the knee.'

'How far above the knee?' She couldn't stop now.

'I haven't got the measurements, Annie. Does it really matter?' He turned away to the window.

A nurse came; there was a telephone call for them. It was Mrs Dyer, from the stables. She asked about Grace, but she was calling about Pilgrim. Logan was with him. Pilgrim was very badly hurt. So Logan thought that they should shoot him. Did Annie agree?

Annie surprised herself again.

'No,' she said angrily. 'No! I want that horse to live. It doesn't matter what it costs. Don't let that man kill him!'

Day after day, Robert and Annie sat in turn at their daughter's hospital bedside. She couldn't move or talk; she lay somewhere between life and death. While one parent watched, the other slept.

Grace Maclean lay in her own little world. She was fed through a hole in her neck. The doctors moved her arms and legs to keep them strong. Robert and Annie left her room together only once, when they went to church. They were present at the service which marked the end of Judith's short life.

Then, one day, Annie was holding her daughter's hand in her own when she saw Grace's finger move. She watched closely, but the movement was not repeated.

'Grace?' she said quietly. 'Grace?'

Nothing. She looked up at the screens above the bed. The speed of Grace's heartbeat was faster, she was sure. Yesterday it was 70. And now 84. She held Grace's hand more tightly in her own. Ninety, a hundred, a hundred and ten . . .

'Talk to her.' A young doctor was standing behind her now.

For a moment, Annie didn't know what to say.

'Grace, it's me. It's time to wake up now. Please wake up.'

◆

The water was warm and thick, and Grace was swimming in it. Far away there was a spot of light. She could go towards it, or turn away, back into the darkness.

Then she heard voices. One, she knew, was her mother's. The other was a man's, but not her father's. She tried to move towards them, but the water was too thick. She tried to call for help, but she couldn't find her voice. She had to try again.

Chapter 2   Grace and Pilgrim

'Did you get the tree?' Annie asked Robert, when he arrived back from town. It was two days before Christmas, and they were preparing for Grace's first short visit home from hospital.

'Yes, I did. Last year's was better, but this one's pretty too.'

'Let's put the lights on it tonight, then.'

'Without Grace?' Robert asked in surprise. 'You know we always do that with her.'

'Don't be stupid!' she cried angrily. 'How can she help when she's only got one leg?'

'Annie, please . . . She'll be OK.'

'No, Robert, she won't be OK. You want it all to be the same, but it can't be the same. Just try and understand that, will you!'

She stood for a moment, her eyes wide and angry. Then she turned and left the room. And Robert knew, deep in his heart, that she was right. Things were never going to be the same again.

◆

While she waited for her parents, Grace looked down at her empty trouser leg. You could feel an arm or a leg after it was gone. She remembered reading that somewhere, and it was true. She could feel the bottom of her leg right now. In fact it was aching terribly. But the funny half-leg that was left didn't seem to belong to her at all.

Judith was dead. And Gulliver. She knew that now, but she tried not to think about it. Pilgrim was fine, though, her father said. She felt better when she heard that. Pilgrim's photograph on the table next to her bed was the first thing that she saw each morning. She looked at it again now. She wasn't going to ride him again, not ever. She wanted to see him one more time, to say goodbye. But that was all.

◆

Pilgrim came home for Christmas too, a week earlier than Grace. Joan Dyer arrived at Logan's stables to collect him. She couldn't believe the change in him. The cuts on his face and chest were

7

bad enough, but he was acting very strangely.

They got him into the trailer with great difficulty, but he kicked angrily against the sides all the way back to the farm.

'I can't put him with the other horses. It won't be safe,' Joan said to Logan.

They drove around to an old empty building and backed the trailer up to the door. But Pilgrim refused to come out. In the end Joan sent her two sons into the trailer with sticks. When Pilgrim finally entered the building, they shut the door quickly. They left the horse kicking wildly against the wooden walls.

◆

Christmas at the Macleans' started badly and got worse.

'Can we put the tree up when we get back?' Grace asked on the drive home from the hospital.

Robert looked quickly at his wife. But Annie did not take her eyes off the road in front of her, and Robert had to explain.

'Baby, we did it last night. You'll want to rest when you get home.'

Grace sat back in her seat and looked out of the window. They continued their journey in silence.

Christmas Day came and went. Grace showed little interest in the hundreds of presents that she received from friends of the family. But her eyes lit up when she saw the gift from her father and mother – a large glass bowl full of small colourful fish. That evening, when Annie finished clearing away dinner, she found Grace and Robert in front of it. They were lying on the floor in the dark. Grace was asleep in her father's arms.

At breakfast the next morning, Grace looked very pale. Robert put his hand on hers.

'Are you all right, baby?'

She looked first at him and then at her mother.

'It's about Pilgrim,' she said slowly. 'I think we should send him back. Back to Kentucky, where you got him from.'

There was a silence.

'Gracie,' Robert began. 'We don't need to decide now. It's too soon . . .'

'I know what you're going to say. Please – I won't ride him again. I know I won't. I can't.' She was crying now. 'And I don't want to see anyone riding him around here.'

Her father held her hand tightly. He was telling her that he understood. He didn't agree, but he understood.

'I want to say goodbye to him first, though. Can we see him this morning before I go back to the hospital?'

◆

Mrs Dyer came out of the stables when they drove up to the house. She looked unhappy about the visit.

'Grace would like to see Pilgrim,' said Robert. 'Is he in the stables?'

'No, he's round the back,' Mrs Dyer answered nervously.

It was clear to Annie and Grace that something was wrong.

'Great,' said Robert. 'Can we see him?'

'Of course.'

They came closer to the old building and Mrs Dyer stopped.

'I don't know if this is a good idea–' she started, but Grace interrupted her.

'I want to see him. Please open the door.'

Mrs Dyer opened it. It took a few moments for the girl's eyes to find her horse in the darkness of the building.

'Pilgrim? Pilgrim?'

Then she saw him. She gave a sudden cry and turned away. Robert reached out quickly to stop her falling.

'No! Oh no!' she shouted.

He put his arm around her and led her away.

'Annie,' Mrs Dyer said. 'I'm so sorry.'

Annie moved towards the door. The smell was terrible. Pilgrim was against a wall in the far corner, watching her. He stood with his neck hanging low; his head was almost touching the ground. The terrible cuts on his face pulled his mouth back, showing his teeth. Annie looked into his bloody, crazy eyes and felt very, very frightened.

Chapter 3   Tom Booker

Even long ago there were men who understood horses. These men could calm the most troubled animals just by talking to them. Nobody knew their secrets, but they were called 'whisperers'.

Annie was in the library. She was reading about a man called Solomon Rarey, from Groveport in Ohio. The British queen, Queen Victoria, heard about his skill with horses, and in 1858 she asked him to come to London. The wildest horse in the country was found and Rarey went into a stable alone with him. Three hours later, Rarey came out leading the horse. The horse followed him like a lamb.

Annie read about a lot of other, similar cases, but in her mind all the horses had one face – Pilgrim's. While she walked back to her office, she thought about Grace. Physically, she was getting better: she could walk quite well now with the help of a stick. But something was wrong inside. Grace tried to hide it from all of them – her family, her friends, her doctors. But Annie could see that something inside her daughter was slowly dying.

Why did she think that the life of a damaged horse was so important to Grace's future happiness? Annie did not mind that Grace did not want to ride again. In fact, she was happy about it. But why could she not let the poor animal die? Where did you look for someone with the special skills of a whisperer?

Then she saw him.

When she returned home that night, Robert and Grace were asleep. Standing in the doorway of Grace's room, Annie had a sudden thought. She needed to find someone to calm Pilgrim's troubled heart. But perhaps this need wasn't about Grace at all. Perhaps it was about herself.

She pulled the bedcovers up over Grace's shoulders and walked back to the kitchen. There was a message on the table from Harry Logan. He had the name of a man who could, possibly, help.

◆

Tom Booker was in California, hundreds of miles from his Montana home, at a clinic for nervous horses and their even more nervous owners. He was getting tired of the same old problems, year after year. The horses were never the problem, he thought. The problem was their less intelligent owners. Perhaps he was too old for these clinics. He was forty-five now, nearly forty-six. He just wanted to go home and spend time on his ranch.

'He doesn't listen to me,' a woman was saying to him. 'When I tell him to move faster, for example.'

Tom watched the horse. He thought before he spoke.

'The horse isn't stupid or crazy. He's frightened. Perhaps while you're telling him one thing, your body's saying something different. Do you kick him to make him go?'

'Yes, I have to.'

'And then you feel that he's going too fast. So you pull him back?'

'Yes, sometimes,' she replied.

'Sometimes. I see. And then he throws you off?'

The woman was beginning to understand. He worked with the horse for about an hour, letting him run on the end of the rope. He played with him, talking softly to him. By the end of the

12

hour the horse was following all his instructions. When he returned the horse to the owner, the woman was almost in tears. She walked slowly and nervously to the animal and touched its neck.

'Don't worry,' said Tom. 'They're the most forgiving animals. They want to please you. But when the messages get mixed up, they can only try to save themselves.'

◆

Many years ago Tom's father, Daniel Booker, worked the land in Montana like his father and grandfather before him. From the day that he was born, Tom was around horses. His parents often found the small boy asleep in the stables with them. His father and grandfather had a special understanding of horses, and Tom learned from them.

'It's like asking a woman to dance,' the old man often said. Tom's grandfather was a great dancer. 'You're frightened that she's going to refuse you. But if you show your fear, then she *will* refuse you. And if she doesn't want to dance, she won't enjoy it. So *you* won't enjoy it.

'Dancing and riding, it's the same thing. It's about trust. You've got to move together. And you've both got to *want* to do it.'

Tom understood these things from the time that he was a small boy. He understood the language of horses. He knew their thoughts and feelings. He and his family went on long rides and slept out under the stars in the springtime. Those were his best memories of his young life.

'Why can't now continue for ever?' his brother Frank said on one of those beautiful moonlit nights.

'Perhaps that's all that for ever is,' his father replied. 'Just one now after another. You can only try to live one now at a time. You can't worry too much about the last now or the next now.'

It seemed to Tom a good way to live your life.

♦

When they had money troubles, the family moved to a smaller ranch at the foot of the Rocky Mountains. Tom helped his parents move, and then left home. He worked for many years on different ranches in Wyoming and Nevada. There he met people who fought with their horses. He met people who beat them. Tom always offered to work with these difficult and frightened animals. At first people thought that he was crazy. They changed their minds, though, when they saw his results.

People started asking for help with their horses and he never refused. His parents could not understand why he earned nothing from this work. His answer was, 'But I don't do it for the people. I do it for the horses.'

To the surprise of his family, Tom then decided to go to university in Chicago. There he met Rachel, a fashionable music student. Eighteen months later, he was back at his parents' ranch with his new wife. Not long after that their son, Hal, was born.

Tom loved them both deeply, but during that first winter the differences between Tom and Rachel became clear. Rachel's world was a world of music, dancing, cinema and books. She could not live in Tom's world and he could not live in hers. When spring came, Rachel took Hal away to the east coast. Tom kissed them both goodbye. Then he started his clinics.

♦

At the end of the first day of the Californian clinic, Tom returned to the hotel. He called home and spoke to his brother.

'There was a call from a woman in New York,' Frank told him.

'What did she want?'

'She didn't say. She just said that it was important.'

Tom put the telephone down. He looked at his watch. It was 10.30, so it was 1.30 in the morning in New York. He got into bed and turned off the light.

At 5.15 he woke to the sound of the telephone.

'Is that Tom Booker?'

'I think so. It's very early.'

'I know, I'm sorry. I wanted to catch you before you left. My name's Annie Maclean. I understand that you help people with horse problems?'

'No, Mrs Maclean, I don't. I help horses who've got people problems.'

He asked her to explain. He listened for a long time in silence while she told him about Pilgrim and Grace.

'That's terrible,' he said finally. 'I'm really sorry. But I can't come to New York. I'm going back to my ranch when the clinic finishes.'

'Please don't say no. Think about it until tomorrow.' It wasn't a question.

The next morning, a package arrived for Tom. It contained a photograph of a girl on a beautiful black horse, and a return ticket to New York.

◆

The chance of seeing his son made Tom decide to go to New York. Hal was a young man now, a student at film school with a part-time job in a restaurant. After an hour or two with Hal, Tom caught a train to Hudson Station. He was early for his meeting with Annie, but he wanted to see the horse alone first.

He took a taxi from the station to Mrs Dyer's place. When the car reached the entrance to the stables, he asked the driver to wait. He introduced himself to Mrs Dyer and asked to see Pilgrim. Then he followed her to the old building behind the stables.

'He's in here?' he asked in surprise.

'Yes. You'll understand when you see him.'

Tom opened the door slowly. The smell was unbelievable.

'Doesn't anyone clean this place?'

'We're all too frightened,' she replied quietly.

He saw Pilgrim through the darkness, his ears flat and his yellow teeth showing. Suddenly the horse jumped towards him, kicking crazily. Tom moved away and closed the door quickly.

'How can you keep him like this? I've never seen anything like it. It's terrible,' he said angrily.

'I know, I've tried to tell . . .'

But he was already moving away. While he was walking across in front of the stables, Mrs Dyer's two boys were beating a horse with sticks. They were trying to get it into a trailer. Tom ran up to one of the boys, took him by the neck and threw him to the ground. Then he reached out for the other boy, took the stick from his hand and held his arm behind his back.

'Don't ever do that to a horse again!' he shouted.

He walked angrily towards the taxi. Just then an expensive silver car stopped next to it.

'Mr Booker?' the driver said. All he remembered about her later were her dark red hair and her sad green eyes. 'I'm Annie Maclean. You got here early.'

'No, Mrs Maclean. I got here much too late.'

He jumped into the taxi, and told the driver to go.

Chapter 4   The Journey West

Annie got the story from the Dyer boys. And their mother told her coldly that she wanted Pilgrim out of the place by Monday. Harry Logan was prepared to keep Pilgrim in his stables for two weeks.

It was three days before Annie was able to speak to Tom Booker.

'Don't ever do that to a horse again!'

'Mr Booker, I want to say how sorry I am . . . about the stables . . . about Pilgrim.'

Tom said nothing.

'We've moved him to another place, a better place. Please, please come and see him again.'

'Mrs Maclean, you've got to understand. That horse is suffering too much. It's wrong to keep him like that.'

'So you think I should let him die?'

'Yes, I do. But of course he's not my horse.'

He refused to make another visit, and she could not change his mind. Finally, she thanked him and ended the conversation.

The lights in the sitting room were off. She walked slowly to the window and stood there for a long time. She looked towards the buildings on the East Side of the city. Ten thousand windows, little spots of light in the night sky. Inside every one of them was a different life with its own special pain.

She knew now what she was going to do. But she didn't want to tell Robert or Grace yet. She had to make some preparations first.

◆

Crawford Gates was the owner of the magazine that Annie worked for. He seemed happy for Annie to go to Montana. It was not a holiday. She was going to take her computer, and she planned to work there. But she knew that her boss was a hard man. He was only interested in his business. And a lot of people were jealous of her position, so it was dangerous to leave the office.

She rented a house in Choteau, a town near Tom Booker's ranch, and found the address of a stable just outside town. Then she was ready to tell Robert and Grace. She was not worried about this. They always agreed to her plans in the end. Tom Booker didn't need to know. She was going to arrive at his ranch, with the horse, after a journey across seven states. He had to see her then.

◆

Grace's feelings about her mother were mixed. She loved her but often felt angry with her. Her mother was always so sure about everything. She knew Grace's likes and dislikes. She understood her hopes and her pain. Sometimes this understanding made Grace feel good. But more often she felt crowded by her mother.

Now, though, at last, she discovered a way to make her mother feel bad. She protected herself by saying nothing. Her silence hurt Annie, and that made Grace feel good.

Annie, Grace and Pilgrim drove west to the Missouri, then followed the wide brown river north to Sioux City. Here they entered South Dakota and headed west again. They travelled without speaking. The sadness between them seemed to grow in this hard, unforgiving land.

One night, they stopped at a small hotel. There were two large beds, side by side, and Grace threw herself down on the one farthest from the door. Annie went out to look after Pilgrim.

She could not let Pilgrim leave the trailer. But after days on the road, the horse no longer acted crazily when Annie opened the door. He just moved back into the darkness and watched. He never touched his food and water until she left.

'Grace?' Annie said softly, when she got back to the room. 'Don't you want to eat?'

No reply. Annie knew that Grace wasn't really asleep. But she didn't want to eat alone, so she decided to go to bed.

That night Annie dreamed that she was walking with her father along a snowy mountain top. They were tied together and there were steep walls of ice on each side of them. Her father turned to smile at her. It's safe, his smile told her. But then the ice opened and he began to fall into the cold darkness below. To save herself and him, she jumped off the other side of the mountain. But the rope did not hold her. She continued to fall helplessly, down, down, down.

It was late afternoon the next day when they drove into the state of Montana. Annie was angry at the weight of Grace's silence and could not hide her feelings. She turned off the main road and stopped the car.

She could feel Grace's eyes on her back, but she did not turn to look at her.

'How long is this going to continue, Grace?'

'What?'

'You know what I mean. How long is it going to continue?' Silence. Annie turned round. 'Is this it now? We've come nearly 2,000 miles and you haven't spoken a word. I just want to know. Is this the way that you and I are going to be now?'

'I don't know,' replied Grace, looking at the floor.

'Do you want to turn around? Shall we go back home?' Grace gave a small laugh. 'Well, shall we?'

Grace lifted her eyes and looked out of the window.

'Because if that's what you want—'

Suddenly Grace turned to her.

'Why are you asking me now?' she shouted. 'You decide! You always do! You're not interested in what other people want! You never listen to anybody!'

'Grace,' Annie said quietly, putting a hand out. But Grace pushed it away.

'Don't! Just leave me alone!'

Annie looked at her for a moment. Then she opened the door and got out. She walked until she came to the top of a hill. Then she stopped and sat down. She began to cry. She cried for Grace and Pilgrim. She cried for the other babies she tried to carry inside her – the babies that were never born. And she cried for herself.

She never felt that she belonged anywhere. America was not her home. But England, where she grew up, did not feel like home now. In each country they thought that she came from the other one. She had no home. Not since her dear father's death.

In some ways, this was useful. She could change to suit the situation. She loved her work, and she was good at it. But since Grace's accident, this all seemed so unimportant. She was being strong for Grace, she thought. But really, she knew no other way to act. She didn't understand herself; and now she did not know her child. She needed action to solve her problems, because she could not live with her feelings. This crazy journey halfway across America was the result.

She cried, holding her head in her hands, until her shoulders hurt. And she stayed there while the sun went down behind the mountains. When she finally looked up, it was night.

'Excuse me!' It was a police officer. 'Are you all right there?'

Annie dried her face and got up.

'Yes. Thank you. I'm fine.'

'Your daughter was worried about you.'

'Yes, I'm sorry. I'm going now.'

She walked back down the hill. Grace's eyes were closed. Annie started the car and turned on the lights. Then she drove through the night, all the way to Choteau.

Chapter 5   New Hope

Two small rivers ran through the Booker brothers' land. They came down from the mountains together, side by side. Then the northern river ran in a straight line through the hills. The southern one moved here and there across flatter land.

The house that they called the river house stood on a hill above the north river. Tom and Rachel lived here after their marriage, then later Frank and Diane. Now it was empty. From it you could look along the river to the ranch house, where Frank's family, and Tom, lived now. Tom looked up at the river house. He thought, not for the first time, about moving into it again.

He and Joe were on their way back from feeding the cattle. They drove down to the ranch and parked near the stables. Joe's younger brothers, Scott and Craig, came running from the house.

'Are you going to see Bronty's baby?' they shouted. 'Can we come?'

He took them into the stables. Bronty was a big ten-year-old horse with a red-brown coat. She pushed her head towards Joe, who had an easy, confident way with horses.

'He looks so funny,' said Scott, watching the young horse behind Bronty.

Tom and Joe let the horses out into the fields, and then turned to walk back to the house.

'Is your mother having visitors?' asked Tom, seeing a silver car coming over the hill.

'I don't know,' replied Joe.

When the car stopped, Tom looked at the driver's face. Joe saw his uncle's surprise.

'You know her?'

'I believe I do. But I don't know what she's doing here.'

Annie got out of the car and walked nervously towards him. She was wearing trousers and boots and a long white top that came halfway down her legs. The sun shone on her red hair and Tom remembered those green eyes from that day at the stables.

'Mr Booker. Good morning.'

'Well, good morning.' They stood for a moment. 'This is Joe, my brother's boy.'

'Hello, Joe. How are you?'

'Fine.'

'What a beautiful place,' she said, looking around.

'It is,' replied Tom.

There was a longer silence. Then she began.

'Mr Booker, you're going to think I'm crazy. But you can guess why I'm here. It's about my daughter's horse. I know you can help him. I came here to ask you to take another look at him.'

'Mrs Maclean—'

'Please. Just a look. It won't take long.'

Tom laughed. 'What, to fly to New York?'

'No. He's here. In Choteau.'

'You've driven him all the way here? Alone?'

Joe was looking from one face to the other, trying to understand. Diane came out of the house. She stood at the door, watching them.

'With Grace, my daughter.'

'Just so I can take a look at him?'

'Yes.'

'Are you coming in to eat, Tom?' Diane called suddenly.

'Tell your mother I'm coming, Joe.'

Tom continued to look at Annie, while she looked at him.

'Excuse me for saying it,' he said. 'But you can't accept no for an answer, can you?'

'No,' Annie said simply. 'You're right. I can't.'

◆

Grace refused to go up to the Booker ranch with Annie. After her mother left, she went out into the little town. Choteau was just one long main street, really. She walked slowly, using her stick. She was not confident yet on her new false leg. People stopped in the street to watch her. When she got back to the cold, lonely house again she felt very unhappy. She lay on her bed and cried.

Annie was excited when she returned from the ranch. She

23

told Grace that Tom Booker was going to have a look at Pilgrim. But Grace showed no interest.

Grace's feelings about Pilgrim were unclear even to herself. In fact they frightened her. She did not want to think about him, but her mother never let her forget. Annie was trying so hard, and Pilgrim wasn't even hers. Of course Grace wanted him to get better, but . . . For the first time she thought that perhaps she didn't want him to get better. Perhaps she wanted him to be like her, damaged for ever. No, stop it, stop it, she told herself. It was crazy to think like this. But why couldn't her mother leave her alone?

'Grace? Are you ready? He'll be here soon.'

Grace didn't reply.

'Grace?'

'Yes? So what?'

She knew the pain she was giving to her mother. It pleased her.

◆

'If you're looking for trouble, you've come to the right place,' said the owner of the stables. 'It nearly killed me getting that crazy horse in.'

Tom could hear Pilgrim kicking the door of the old stable.

The horse looked worse than he remembered. How could he even stand when his front leg was so thin? But here he was, kicking like a wild animal.

Tom drove to Annie's house and pushed the bell. He was surprised at the angry face of the girl who answered the door.

'I guess you're Grace,' he said, smiling. She didn't smile back; she just opened the door wider.

'She's on the telephone. You can wait in here.'

Tom followed Grace into the sitting room. While she was in front of him, he looked down at her leg and her stick. The television was on in the room. Grace sat down and seemed to be watching it. But Tom knew that she wanted him to feel unwelcome.

'What does your mother do?' he asked her.

'What?'

'Your mother. What kind of work does she do?'

'She works for a magazine.'

'That sounds like hard work.'

Grace laughed. It was such an angry laugh that he was surprised again.

'Listen,' Grace said. 'I don't know if she's told you . . . I don't want to know anything about this, OK? It was all her idea. I think it's crazy. They should just let him die.'

She returned to the television. Tom looked out of the window thoughtfully.

'I'm sorry. It was a work call – it was important.'

He turned. Annie's hair was pulled back from her face, wet from a bath. It made her look boyish.

'That's OK.'

'You've been to see him?'

'Yes, I just came from there,' he replied.

'And?'

'Well,' he began, 'he's in a bad state.'

He didn't know how he was going to tell her. Then, over her shoulder, he saw Grace in the doorway. She was trying to look uninterested. He knew, though, that she was listening. He suddenly understood how the three of them – the mother, the daughter and the horse – were all joined in suffering. If he could help the horse, perhaps he could help them all. What was wrong with that? And how could he walk away from such pain?

He heard himself say, 'Perhaps we can do something.'

Hope shone from Annie's eyes.

'Now wait a minute. I said perhaps. But I need to know

something first. It's a question for Grace here.'

Grace looked at him.

'You see, when I work with a horse, the owner's got to be there too. So this is what I'm offering. I'm not sure I can do anything with old Pilgrim. But I'll try if you help me.'

Grace looked away. Annie looked at the floor.

'You have a problem with that, Grace?' Tom said.

Her voice was low when she replied, 'Do you really have to ask?' She left the room again.

'Right. I have to go now.'

He walked towards the door. Annie ran after him.

'What does she have to do?' asked Annie.

'Just be there, help me.'

He put his hat on and opened the front door.

'It's cold in here,' he said. 'Is there something wrong with the heating?'

He was on his way out when he saw Grace in the sitting-room doorway. She spoke very quietly, without looking at him.

'I'm sorry, Grace?'

'I said OK. I'll do it.'

◆

'Why did she just come out here like that? Who does she think she is?' Diane was angry, and Tom couldn't understand why. 'And what about your other work? You said no more clinics!'

'That's enough, Diane. Leave him alone,' Frank told her.

Diane was a tall, strong woman of about forty-five. She was Tom's friend before she met Frank. They went out a few times, but he didn't want any more than that. So Diane married the younger brother, Frank. Tom liked her a lot. He worried sometimes, though, that she was spending more time on him than on Frank. But Frank never seemed to mind.

'Is the girl's leg made of wood?' Scott said through a mouth

'I said OK. I'll do it.'

full of food.

'Just eat your food, Scott,' said Frank.

They ate in silence for a few minutes.

Tom and Frank worked well together. The two of them were close, and they never disagreed about the ranch. Frank was a better businessman and knew much more about cattle than his brother. Tom did his clinics and looked after the horses. Frank was happy with that.

'Is the woman famous?' It was Scott again.

Diane didn't give Tom the chance to answer.

'Have you heard of her?' she asked the boy.

'No.'

'Well then, she isn't famous, is she? Eat your food.'

Chapter 6   Understandings

From the top of the hill you could see right down to the ranch below. Tom saw Annie's car turning in front of the ranch house. Two people got out of the car. They were far away, but Tom had a clear picture of Annie in his mind. 'Stop thinking about her. She's another man's wife,' he told himself. But he couldn't get her out of his thoughts.

It was cattle-branding day at the ranch. A lot of friends and neighbours were there to help. The young animals made a terrible noise when the heated metal burned into their skins. Tom could see that Annie and Grace didn't like it. So he quickly found a job for Annie and took Grace off with him. Later Annie saw Grace at the front of the branding line. Tom was showing her what to do. To begin with, she kept her eyes closed.

'Not too hard,' she heard him say. Grace touched the red–hot metal on the animal's back and the smell of burning was terrible. 'That's good. It hurts him, but not for long. There . . . look at that

. . . Grace, that's a perfect brand. The best of the day.'

The girl's face was red and her eyes were shining with excitement. People around her called out and she laughed and joked with them. Tom saw Annie watching and smiled at her.

'Your turn next, Annie.'

◆

When it was finished, everyone went up to the house to eat. Annie felt that it was time to leave. She saw Grace walking to the house with Joe in easy conversation. Annie called her name.

'We have to go now,' Annie said.

'What? Why?'

'Yes, why?' It was Tom.

'Well, you know, it's getting late.'

'Yes. And you've got to get back to work on that computer and make all those telephone calls, right?'

The sun was behind him and Annie put her head on one side and looked at him. Men didn't usually make fun of her like this. She enjoyed it.

'It's the same every year here, you see. The person who does the best brand has to make a speech after dinner.'

'What!' said Grace.

'So, Grace, you go in and get yourself ready. Joe, why don't you show her the way?'

'If you're sure we're invited . . .' said Annie.

'You're invited,' replied Tom.

'Thank you.'

'You're welcome.'

They both smiled. The silence between them was filled for a few moments by the sounds of the cattle.

Diane was never very friendly towards Annie. Today, though, she made her feel welcome.

The children sat together at one end of the table. They talked

29

so loudly in their excitement that the adults could only just hear themselves speak.

Joe was telling Grace about a strange woman who lived up on the mountains.

'She's got these Pryor Mountain horses and just lets them run wild. There are quite a lot of them now. And it's the same with her children. They run around with nothing on. Came here from Los Angeles.'

Then Annie heard Grace telling Joe about her friends in New York.

Later, when the meal was coming to an end, Frank said, 'You know what, Tom? While you're working on that horse of theirs, Annie and Grace could live in the river house. It seems crazy for them to do all that driving to and from Choteau.'

'Sure,' Tom agreed. 'Good idea.'

'Oh, that's very nice of you, but really . . .'

'Come on, Annie. I know that house in Choteau. It's in a terrible state.'

'But Frank, you know the river house isn't much better,' said Diane. 'And I'm sure Annie and Grace want to spend time alone together.'

Before Annie could speak, Frank looked along the table.

'Grace? What do you think?'

Grace looked at Annie, but her face gave her answer. It was all that Frank needed.

'That's agreed then.'

Diane suddenly got up. 'I'll make some coffee,' she said.

◆

Pilgrim ran into the arena like a shot. He went straight to the far end and stopped there in a cloud of red sand. His ears moved nervously, and his eyes were wild. But he watched the open gate. He knew that the man was coming in through it.

30

Tom was on foot and carried an orange flagstick and a rope. He came in and shut the gate. Then he walked to the centre of the arena.

For almost a minute they stood there. The horse looked at the man, and the man looked at him. It was Pilgrim who moved first. He lowered his head and took some small steps back. Tom stayed in the same place, not moving. The end of the flagstick was resting on the sand. Then he took a step towards Pilgrim and at the same time lifted the flag in his right hand. The horse ran to the left.

Round and round the arena he went. He was making a lot of noise and throwing his head up and down. But his eyes never left the man. They were held there by a line of fear.

Soon his skin began to shine and water flew from the corners of his mouth. But the man made him continue. Every time he slowed, there was that flag again. He had to keep running.

The horse's leg was strong again now after days of swimming, and his face and chest were looking better. His problem now was inside his head. Pilgrim went past for perhaps the hundredth time; Grace saw him turn his head to look at Tom. Where was that flag? Why was Tom letting him slow down? Pilgrim reduced his speed to a walk and then stopped.

He stood there, looking around him. After a few moments, Tom started to walk towards him. When he was about 14 feet away, Pilgrim ran to the left again. But this time Tom stepped in and stopped him with the flag. The horse paused and ran to the right, and Tom hit him on the back with the flag. He started running around the arena again, the opposite way this time.

'He wants to be all right,' Tom said. 'He just doesn't know what all right is.'

About two hours later, Tom opened the gate and let Pilgrim back into the stable.

Tom and Grace drove back to the ranch together.

'Grace, I've got a problem. When I'm working with a horse, I like to know the history.'

Grace said nothing.

'I can understand if you don't want to talk about it. But I need to understand what Pilgrim's feeling. So I need to know everything about that day.'

Grace didn't want to tell anyone what she really remembered about that day. The problem was Judith. She just couldn't talk about Judith. Or even Gulliver. She looked back at Tom Booker and he smiled kindly.

'I don't mean now,' he said quietly. 'When you're ready. And only if you want to.'

'I'll think about it,' she said.

◆

In New York, Robert arrived back home after another long day at the office. The place seemed so empty without Annie and Grace; he tried not to spend much time there.

The best part of his day was talking to them on the telephone. And tonight, after failing to speak to them all day, he felt a more urgent need for the sound of their voices.

And then he heard the telephone.

'Annie . . . how are things? I tried calling you earlier.'

'I'm sorry. There's only one telephone line in this new place and the office is on it all the time.'

Annie told him about her day. She sounded unhappy and Robert tried to make her feel better.

'And how's Gracie?'

'Oh, I don't know.' Her voice was low now. 'She's fine with Tom Booker and Joe – you know, the twelve-year-old? She and Joe are becoming close friends. But when it's the two of us, I don't know. It's so bad – she doesn't even look at me.'

Robert walked to the window and looked out at the New

Round and round the arena he went.

York night. 'I miss you, Annie.'

'I know,' she said. 'We miss you too.'

◆

The agreement with Crawford Gates was that Annie could be away for a month. It was nearly a month already. She had to ask him for more time. But Gates was beginning to question things that she decided about the magazine. That was worrying her; it was not a good idea to be away from the office for too long. At least the new telephone lines in the river house were going to make it easier to stay in touch. Tom was going to put them in for her.

She was just turning on her computer when she saw him outside her window. Behind him stood two horses, ready to ride.

She looked at him for a moment, smiling. He was smiling too. Perhaps it was the light, but to her his eyes seemed clearer and bluer than ever – like the sky behind him.

'I need your help. I've got all these young horses to ride and poor old Rimrock here is not getting enough exercise. Would you ride him? He's very quiet.'

'Is this how I pay for the telephones?'

He laughed. 'No. But I'll think of something.'

◆

Grace always remembered her dreams. It was easy. You just told someone about them the moment you woke up. You could even tell yourself. When she was a child she always climbed into her parents' bed in the morning. Her father put his arm around her and she told him. It was only her father. Her mother was already up, and calling Grace to her piano practice.

To her surprise, Grace did not often dream about the accident. She did have one dream about Pilgrim. He was standing on the far side of a great brown river. He was younger and very small.

34

She called him and he tested the water with his foot. Then he walked right in and started swimming towards her. But he wasn't strong enough and the water began to carry him away.

She watched his head getting smaller and smaller and she felt so weak and frightened. She called his name again and again. Then she saw someone standing quietly behind her. She turned. It was Tom Booker. He said that she mustn't worry. Pilgrim was going to be all right. Further down, the river wasn't so deep. He could stand up there and climb out.

She decided to tell Tom Booker about the day of the accident.

◆

Tom could see that Annie was a rider; her body moved with the horse. They rode up a long hill to a place where you could look down on the two rivers. They stopped and sat for a while.

'That's a beautiful view,' Annie said.

They could just see the top of the river house.

'Who's R. B.?' she asked. 'I found the letters T. B. – I guess that's you – and R. B. on a tree near the house. So who's R. B.?'

He laughed. 'Rachel. My wife.'

'You're married?'

'Not now. A long time ago. I have a son too – Hal. But Rachel didn't like it here. The winters are hard for city people. So she left, with Hal.'

◆

'I heard the truck when it was a long way away,' said Grace. 'We had all the time in the world, I thought.'

While she told Tom the story of that morning, he watched her closely. He knew she was reliving the death of her friend. He understood how she was feeling. He felt terribly sorry for her.

'I don't know if Judith saw the truck. I think she hit her head really hard on the road. And Gully was going crazy, you know.

But when I saw it coming, I knew it couldn't stop. I thought I could calm Gully. Then I could pull Judith out of the way. I was so stupid!' She held her head in her hands for a few moments.

'Why didn't I get off and just pull Gully away? But I didn't. Pilgrim was great. I mean he was frightened but he seemed to understand. He tried to get near Judith. My fingers were so close to hers ... and then the driver sounded his horn ...'

Grace looked at Tom, the pain showing on her face. Finally the tears came and Tom put his arms around her.

'I saw her face looking up at me, down by Gully's feet. It was just before the noise of the horn. She looked so little, so afraid. And I didn't save her. I let her die!'

Tom didn't speak. For a long time they stood that way until her crying stopped. He asked her if she wanted to continue.

'Pilgrim heard the horn and seemed to go crazy. He turned to face the truck. He didn't want this great thing to hurt us. He wanted to fight it! And when it was right in front of us he lifted his front legs. Then he jumped at it. I fell and hit my head. That's all I can remember ... Will all this help you to help Pilgrim?'

'I hope so,' Tom replied.

◆

Tom was late for supper.

'Is she happy about her new telephones, then?' asked Diane coldly. 'I don't know why she needs three lines – she's only got two ears.'

'She's pleased.'

'Frank says you took her out riding this morning.'

'That's right,' Tom replied. 'She's a good rider.'

Tom didn't want to fight with Diane. He ate his food, checked the horses and went up to his room.

Tom looked through a pile of old magazines. He was looking for something to help him with Pilgrim. He remembered a piece by a Californian man who also worked with horses. He found the right magazine, and read the piece again. If a horse was afraid, it ran away. But when it felt pain, the animal turned to defend itself. That was interesting, but what did it mean? There were no answers, he decided. It was always just you and the horse. You tried to understand its mind, and it tried to understand yours.

Tom pushed the magazine away. And then he suddenly understood the meaning of the fear in Pilgrim's eyes. The horse was lost and alone; since that terrible day, he could trust nobody. Grace, Gulliver, Judith – they led him up that icy path. They told him it was safe. Then they hurt him when it wasn't.

Perhaps Pilgrim also felt bad about his own part in it all. He wanted to protect Grace, but he couldn't. And when he attacked the truck to save her from it, he suffered pain and then, at the Dyers' stable, punishment.

Later, when his light was off and the house was quiet, Tom felt his own fear. He had a clear picture of the darkness of Pilgrim's mind. He wanted so much to help – for the horse, and for the girl. But he knew that most of all he wanted it for the woman with the red hair and sad, green eyes.

Chapter 7 Mother and Daughter

After Matthew Graves's death, his wife sold their house in Jamaica and took Annie to live in England. She left her daughter with the child's grandparents in the country. She went to London and, six months later, married again.

Annie was deeply unhappy. She missed her father terribly. He was the only one who ever made her feel good about herself. Her mother and grandparents thought she was a useless troublemaker. Through school and through her student days, and then through her working life, she was driven by a single purpose

– to show them that they were wrong.

When Grace was born, Annie thought her journey was complete. But then she lost the next baby, and the next, and the next. She felt like that angry girl in her grandparents' home, failing again. She had to be successful at something.

So she became one of the best in her business. And in her present job, on one of the top magazines, she could be cold and hard with others. She won every fight, and the losers left the magazine. She never felt sorry for them.

Now she thought about these things. She thought about the hurt inside her that made her act like that. She looked outside at another world, warm and green on this May morning. But she only felt part of it when she was with Tom.

Every Wednesday Diane collected Grace from the clinic in town, where she practised using her new leg. Sometimes Frank or Diane took her there on other days. On those mornings, Tom often came to the door and invited Annie to ride with him. She always tried not to show too much excitement.

She was already in her riding clothes when he came this morning. While she stood next to him with the horses, she enjoyed the smell of him: a warm, clean smell of leather and soap. The tops of their arms touched lightly, and they didn't move away.

They talked while they rode. He said that a frightened horse often had to get worse before it got better. You had to accept that. And she didn't answer; she knew that he wasn't just talking about Pilgrim. He was talking about all of them.

The night before, she heard Grace on the telephone telling her father about her conversation with Tom. Afterwards Annie waited for Grace to tell her about the conversation, but she didn't. At first Annie was angry with Tom.

'I hear Grace told you about the accident?'

'Yes, she did,' he said. And that was all. It was clear that, for him, the conversation was just between him and Grace. Tom almost never spoke to her about Grace; when he did, it was about safe things, facts. But Annie knew that he could see the problems between the two of them.

◆

Joe and Grace walked towards Pilgrim. She felt comfortable with Joe now. She didn't mind that he walked more slowly to stay at her side.

'He was such a beautiful horse,' she said.

'You mean he *is* a beautiful horse.'

Pilgrim was watching them from the far end of the field.

'So, are you going to ride him?' Joe asked.

'What?' She gave a short laugh.

'I mean, when he's better.'

'Oh, I'm not going to ride him again.'

Joe was quiet for a few moments.

'Pity,' he said. 'We're all going up into the hills soon. We're going to take the cattle to their summer fields. It's good fun.'

They walked back towards the stables.

She could never ride Pilgrim again. He did not need her fear *and* his own. But she could try another horse, perhaps.

'My horse or Rimrock?' asked Joe.

◆

Annie was back from shopping for food for a dinner party. The Bookers were all coming to the river house for a meal in the evening. Annie put the computer on and found a message from Robert on the screen. He wanted to visit them this weekend, but he couldn't. He had to fly to Geneva on business. She couldn't understand why she was secretly pleased about that. Her feelings worried her.

She sat down. Where was Grace? Nobody was at the ranch

when she got back from the shops. Were they all at the arena?

◆

At Grace's speed, it was a ten-minute walk down to the river. She was meeting Joe and the horses there. It was a beautiful spot, hidden from the world by trees. She waited and listened for Joe.

'Did anybody see you?' Grace said, when he finally arrived. This was their secret.

'No.' Joe was on Rimrock, and leading Gonzo. Gonzo was a small, calm horse that Joe often rode.

Grace tried to get on, but she hurt her leg and fell. She cried out angrily.

'Are you OK?' said Joe, helping her up. 'Are you sure about this?'

'Yes. I'm sorry. I just get so angry sometimes.'

Joe held the horse with one hand and offered the other to Grace. Grace put her left hand on Joe's shoulder. She hoped that he couldn't feel her fear. She lifted her new leg over Gonzo. At the same time, Joe pushed her up. To her surprise, she was now sitting on the horse's back.

After a few moments she gave Gonzo a little kick with her good leg. He moved without question and they walked along the river bank. She could do more with the new leg than she thought. She practised moving it. Soon the animal understood what she wanted. When they reached the end of the field, horse and rider were one.

Grace lifted her eyes for the first time and saw Joe watching her. She rode back to him and stopped. He smiled up at her with the sun in his eyes, and Grace suddenly wanted to cry. But she bit hard on the inside of her lip and smiled back at him.

'Easy,' he said.

'Yes,' she said, holding back the tears. 'Easy.'

◆

'Easy,' he said.

It was good to hear the sound of people laughing. The house was, at last, filled with noise. They were all there: Diane, Frank, Tom, Joe, Craig and Scott. The food wasn't so great, but nobody seemed to mind.

After the meal, the children went to play games on Annie's computer. It wasn't long, though, before Scott ran in again.

'Joe isn't letting me use the computer,' he cried to Diane.

'It's not your turn,' Joe called from the other room.

'It is! You never let me have a turn.'

'Don't be such a baby,' Joe said.

'Boys, boys.' Frank tried to calm his sons.

'You think you're so great—' Scott shouted at his brother.

'Oh shut your mouth, Scott,' Joe replied.

'—giving Grace riding lessons and everything.'

Everyone went quiet. Annie looked at Grace, who looked away. Nobody knew what to say.

'I saw you! She was on Gonzo. Down by the river,' Scott continued.

Joe jumped at him, shouting. Then everyone was on their feet. The table, with the coffee cups and the glasses, was turned on its side. Annie and Grace could only stand and watch.

Soon Frank was leading the boys out of the house.

'Annie, I'm so sorry,' Diane said.

Grace stood alone on the other side of the room.

'I'm going upstairs,' she said, picking up her stick. She left the room.

Annie turned to Tom. 'Did you know about this? Did everyone know except me?'

'I don't think any of us knew,' replied Tom.

She just wanted them all to go now. But Tom and Diane stayed to help her with the dishes.

'How's Pilgrim?' Annie asked Tom.

'Oh, I think he'll be fine, Annie. Where there's pain, there's feeling. Where there's feeling, there's hope.'

He turned to face her.

'Thanks,' Annie said quietly.

'That's OK. Don't let her push you away. Keep trying, Annie.'

She watched them walk away into the darkness. She wanted to call Tom back. She wanted him to stay there and hold her. To keep her from the cold that was falling once again over that house.

◆

He wanted her more than any woman since Rachel. He thought about her now while he looked out at the night sky. Perhaps she felt the same. She seemed to smile at him in a special way; when she spoke, her words always seemed to be for him. He wanted to take her in his arms and make her feel better. But he also wanted to know the feel and the shape and the smell of her.

◆

When Annie opened Grace's bedroom door, the light from the stairs filled the room. Grace was in bed, with her face to the wall.

'Grace?'

No answer.

'Grace?'

'What?' She didn't move.

'Can we talk?'

'I want to go to sleep.'

'So do I. I think we should talk, though.'

Grace turned over on her back.

'What about?'

Slowly now, Annie told herself. Get it right.

'So you're riding again. How was it?'

'OK.'

'That's great.'

'Is it? Why?'

Don't get angry, Annie said to herself. She continued:

'Why didn't you tell me?'

'You?' Grace shouted. 'Why do *you* need to know? Because you're interested? Or just because you have to know everything? Because nobody can do anything without your agreement? You didn't *want* me to ride again. I hate you. Get out! Leave me alone! Get out!'

Annie walked slowly to the door. Her heart was beating fast. Then she heard a sound behind her.

'What?' she said.

She waited. There was something about Grace's voice. Annie knew that she had to go back to her.

'I said . . . nobody's ever going to want me,' Grace said in a small voice. Her face was wet with tears.

'Oh Grace, that's not true.'

'What have I got that anyone's going to want?'

'You're you. You're special and you're beautiful. And you're the strongest person I know.'

She held her daughter tightly, and they both cried.

Annie couldn't tell how long they sat there. But it was long after their crying stopped. Grace fell asleep in her arms. She put her down again on the bed and lay down next to her. Then she slept too, a deep and dreamless sleep.

Chapter 8   Annie and Tom

Grace saw the smile on his face when she climbed into the car. She knew that today was in some way special.

'You're early,' she said.

'Am I?' He looked at his watch. 'Probably something wrong with this thing again.'

44

'You're you. You're special and you're beautiful.'

There was a rope on the back seat, an unusual purple and green one.

'What's that for?' asked Grace.

'Oh, it's useful for all kinds of things.'

When they got to the arena, Tom picked up the rope and went in. Pilgrim moved away to his usual place in the far corner. But Tom didn't look at him. He was doing something with the rope while he walked. Grace couldn't see what it was. He came to a stop in the centre of the arena.

Pilgrim stopped walking and looked at Tom. He threw his head up several times. Tom turned his back to the horse and started playing with the rope. He looked up and smiled at Grace.

'He wants to know what I'm doing. Am I right?' he asked.

She looked across at Pilgrim. The horse took a few small steps to get a better look. Tom heard him and moved further away. This was repeated a number of times until the horse and man were much closer than before.

'Are you going to try to put that rope on him?' she asked. She couldn't believe it.

'Only if he asks me to.'

Horse and man continued the dance. Every time Pilgrim came closer, Tom moved away. At last Tom could feel the animal's heat on the back of his neck.

He moved suddenly and Pilgrim jumped. But he didn't move away. For the first time, Tom was looking straight at him. The horse could see the rope. Tom was saying something, but Grace couldn't hear his words. 'Go on, Pilgrim,' she thought. 'Go to him. He won't hurt you.'

Pilgrim went slowly towards the rope. He put his nose to it and smelt it. Then he moved to Tom's hands and smelt them too. Tom just stood there and let him.

At that moment Grace felt many things come together. She couldn't explain it, even to herself. She was friends with her mother again. She was riding. She felt good with people. Before today she was afraid of losing all that again. But Pilgrim's show of trust changed everything. She knew now that the change in herself was going to stay with her for ever.

Pilgrim let Tom place a hand on his head. Then, calmly and very slowly, Tom put the rope around his neck.

He knew how Grace was feeling; he didn't have to look at her. But she didn't know yet that this was just the beginning. There was more work, difficult work, to do. But not today.

He called her into the arena and she walked slowly towards them. When she was close, Tom told her to stop. The horse had to come to her.

He could see Grace biting her lip. She held her hands out below the horse's nose. There was fear on both sides. Then Pilgrim put his nose to her hands, and to her face and hair.

◆

Grace was telling Robert that, in two days' time, she was going to help with the cattle drive. They were taking them up into the hills. Yes, she said, of course she was going to ride there.

'You don't have to worry. Gonzo's fine.'

Annie went to stand at Grace's shoulder.

'No, she's not coming,' Grace said to Robert. 'She says she's got too much to do. She's right here. Do you want to talk to her? OK. I love you too.'

She handed Annie the telephone and went upstairs for a bath. Robert was in Geneva on business, but he was returning to New York in a few days. He listened in silence while Annie told him the news from her office.

'Gates has told Lucy to leave! I can't accept that. I employed her soon after I started the job. What shall I do?'

'Well, from Montana there's not much that you *can* do.'

'Are you saying we should come back?'

47

'No, I'm not saying that.'

'When everything's going so well with Grace and Pilgrim?'

'No, Annie, I didn't say that.'

'That's what it sounded like.'

There was a silence on the other end.

'I'm sorry, Annie,' he said slowly. 'It's important that you all stay there – if you need to.'

They talked about other things. They were friends again when they said goodbye. But this time he didn't tell her he loved her. Annie put the telephone down and sat there.

Suddenly she knew what she had to do. Gates had to give Lucy her job back. If he refused, she didn't want to work for him any more. She wrote him a letter. While she was waiting for an answer, she was going to go on the cattle drive.

◆

Through the flames of the open fire, Annie watched the children's faces and their shining eyes. Grace looked beautiful, she thought.

'Do your rope trick,' Scott said to Tom.

Tom smiled and pulled something from his pocket. It was a piece of thin rope about two feet long. He tied the ends together and made a loop. 'OK,' he said. 'This one's for Annie.' He came towards her and fell on his knees in front of her.

'Hold up the first finger of your right hand,' he told her. He put the loop over it. Holding the other end of the loop tight with his left hand, he put one side of the rope over the other with the middle finger of his right hand. Then he turned the hand over; now it was under the loop. Then he turned it back again and brought the ends of his fingers to Annie's.

It seemed that the loop went around their fingers. To take it off they had to break their touch. They both smiled.

'Look,' Tom said softly.

She looked down again at their fingers. He pulled the rope

slowly and it came away. The loop was in place, though.

Annie tried to do it a few times; Grace, Craig and Scott tried too. But only Joe knew how it was done. Then Tom stood up, took the rope and gave it to Annie.

'Is this a gift?'

'No,' he said. 'Just until you learn how to do the trick.'

◆

She woke. For a moment she had no idea where she was. Then she remembered and looked up at the moon. She turned and saw Grace's sleeping face next to her. She was thirsty. So she got out of her sleeping bag and started walking towards the river. The cattle lifted their heads to look at her.

She walked a little way along the river bank. There she found a place where she could reach the water. She drank from her hands.

She saw him first in the water, when he moved across in front of the moon.

'Are you OK?' he asked.

She smiled. 'I'm fine. I was just thirsty.'

'Does the water taste good?'

'Beautiful. Try it.'

He walked towards her, put his hands to the water and drank.

When he finished drinking, he turned to her. She reached out and brushed the water from his face. And with this touch of her fingers on his face, the world stopped.

He took her hand. He held it softly and kissed it. Then she reached out with her other hand and ran it across the side of his face. He brought his hand up to her face. At his touch she closed her eyes.

Annie felt a sudden need to say sorry. She wanted to ask for his forgiveness. She never planned to do this. But before the idea could become words, he brought his lips to hers. They kissed. It seemed to Annie that she was coming home.

◆

In the morning, over breakfast, Diane told Annie about the surprise that she and Frank had for the children. Next week they were all going to Disneyland.★ She was clearly telling Annie, in a kindly way, that she and Grace should really go home now.

On the ride back to the ranch they saw a group of horses, far away. 'They're the Pryor Mountain horses that Joe was talking about. Do you remember?' Tom said. It was almost the only thing he said to her all day.

There were several messages on the answering machine when she and Grace got home. But two of the messages were more important than the others.

The first was from Crawford Gates. He was not going to take Lucy back. He was sorry that Annie was leaving the magazine. The second message was from Robert. He was flying out to Montana to spend the weekend with them.

Chapter 9   Robert's Visit

Tom stayed away from Annie when he heard about Robert's visit. They spoke very little except on that first evening.

'Diane tells me that they're all going to Los Angeles next week,' Annie said.

'Yes, but the children don't know yet.'

'And you're going to Wyoming.'

'That's right. I promised to look at a few horses down there.'

Tom tried not to show his feelings. He didn't want to make things difficult for her. She probably felt bad about their meeting by the river.

★ Disneyland: a place of family entertainment in Los Angeles

'Is this a gift?'

'I hear that Grace's father is coming this weekend?'

'Yes. Grace is so excited.'

'We'll see if we can get Grace on Pilgrim for him.'

'Really?'

'I don't see why not. I'll try it first. If he's OK with me, Grace can do it for her father.'

'Then we can take him home.' She looked into his eyes.

'Right.'

'Tom—'

'Of course, you're welcome to stay here until you're ready. You don't have to leave just because we're all away.'

She tried to smile. 'Thank you.'

They did not speak again and Tom spent all his time with Pilgrim. At the end of the week, he rode Pilgrim for the first time. He knew that Grace could ride him too now.

◆

There was a small crowd at the airport, but Robert couldn't see Annie or Grace. Then he looked more closely at two women in wide hats. They seemed to be laughing at him. He saw, to his surprise, that it was his wife and daughter.

'Well, well,' he called. 'It's Pat Garrett and Billy the Kid!'★

'What brings you into town, stranger?' said Grace. She took off her hat and threw her arms around his neck.

'My baby, how are you? How *are* you?'

'I'm fine.' She held Robert tightly.

'You are. I can see. Let me look at you.'

He couldn't believe it. He remembered her lying in hospital, sad and empty. Now here she was, full of life and looking happy.

★ Pat Garrett and Billy the Kid: famous nineteenth-century Americans. Billy the Kid was a gunfighter and cattle-stealer. Pat Garrett, a lawman, finally found him and killed him.

'Well, what do you think?' she said to him.

'What do you mean?'

She turned quickly on one foot and he suddenly understood.

'No stick. You little star!'

He gave her a kiss and at the same time reached out for Annie. Her brown skin made her eyes seem clear and so very green. She looked more beautiful than he ever remembered. She stepped in close and put her arms around him. They kissed and Robert held her tightly.

'It seems a very long time,' he said at last.

'I know,' replied Annie.

◆

On the drive back Grace was so happy to see her parents together again. The final pieces of her broken life were falling into place. There was just one other piece. She had to ride Pilgrim.

The thought worried and excited her. She didn't *want* to ride him again. She just knew that she had to. Her worries were not about fear. She worried that she was not good enough for Pilgrim.

Her new leg was now too tight; it was giving her pain all the time. The trouble was that she had to go to New York for a new one. She wasn't ready to go to New York. First she had to ride Pilgrim.

They drove over the hill and saw the ranch in front of them. Annie stopped the car to let Robert enjoy the view.

'Wow,' Robert said. 'Now I know why you don't want to come home.'

◆

Tom wanted to dislike Annie's husband, but Robert was a nice man. Of course he was. He was full of life, funny and interesting. More important, he was interested.

Tom was driving Robert around the ranch. Robert asked Tom a lot of questions about the animals and plants that they saw. Grace made fun of him all the time from the back seat.

Tom thought of Annie and all her questions. She and Robert belonged together. He tried to push that thought out of his mind.

It was raining heavily when he took them back to the river house. Grace stepped out of the car and fell badly. She gave a little cry and Tom jumped out of the front seat.

'Grace, are you OK?' asked her father.

'I'm fine.' She was already trying to get up. 'Really, I'm fine.'

Annie came running out of the house.

'What's the matter?'

'It's OK,' Robert said. 'She fell.'

They helped her to her feet and into the house.

'See you all in the morning, then,' Tom said.

'OK. Thanks for the trip,' Robert answered.

Turning round on his way back to the car, Tom's eyes met Annie's. That short look contained all that their hearts could say.

Tom touched the front of his hat to them and said good night.

◆

Grace knew that her false leg was broken. She stood in the bathroom and looked at the damage. She also knew that she couldn't tell her parents.

She decided what to do. She pulled herself over to the medicine cupboard and got out a box of Band-Aids.* She was going to do her own repairs. Then she was going to practise on Gonzo before she rode Pilgrim.

---

* Band-Aid: a thin band of sticky material that is used to protect a cut on your skin. Band-Aid is one company's name for these pieces of material.

◆

Robert was already in bed, waiting.

'Oh, Annie, I missed you so much.'

'I missed you too.'

'Really?'

'Sssh. Of course.'

He moved his body closer, and she felt his hands on her. She closed her eyes. But she could not stop thinking about Tom, and she felt terrible about that. She knew that this was the end of her marriage. Things were never going to be the same again.

◆

Robert drove Grace down to the stables after breakfast. It was a beautiful clear day and the sky was a sea of blue.

'Are you OK, Grace?'

'You've got to stop asking me that. I'm fine. Please.'

'I'm sorry.'

Joe led them to Gonzo. Robert saw that she was walking with difficulty. Once she had to reach for a gate and wait for a moment.

'No hat?' Robert asked. She was preparing to get on the horse now.

'You mean no hard hat?'

'Well, yes.'

'No, no hat.'

Robert made a face, then smiled. 'You know best.'

Grace narrowed her eyes at him. Joe looked from one to the other and smiled. Then Grace put her hands on the back of the horse and lifted up her good leg. Her weight moved to her false leg, which could not hold it.

'Oh,' she said, clearly in pain.

'What is it?'

55

'Nothing. It's OK.'

But tears began to run down her cheeks.

'Gracie, what is it?'

He thought at first that she was in pain. But when she finally spoke, she was clearly angry too.

'It's no good,' she shouted. 'I can't do it.'

◆

That same afternoon Robert called the clinic in New York. Grace needed a new leg, he told them. Then he tried to get plane tickets for all three of them.

'There's a problem, Annie. There are only two seats.'

There was a silence while Grace and Robert waited for Annie's reply. Robert knew there was something different about her; he couldn't say exactly what. She seemed unhappy. But he told himself that the problem was her job.

Annie was looking out of the window at the perfect late spring afternoon. She turned back to them and pulled a jokey, sad face.

'I'll be all alone here.'

They laughed. Grace put an arm around her.

'Oh, poor little Mother.'

Robert smiled at her. 'Have a holiday. Enjoy it. After a year of Crawford Gates, you need some free time.'

He called the airport again and got tickets for himself and Grace.

◆

Later, the two families came together for a meal by the river. Annie found it hard to look Tom in the eye when he handed a drink to her. Their fingers touched on the glass and her heart missed a beat.

'So, you're staying on the ranch alone next week.'

'It's no good,' she shouted. ' I can't do it.'

'Oh, yes.'

'At least there'll be someone at the end of the telephone if there's a problem,' Diane said.

Annie smiled. 'It's very kind of you. I know our stay is much longer than you thought.'

Diane went off to check the children.

'I'm really sorry about Grace,' Tom said.

'Yes, well. It's not too bad. She can ride Pilgrim when you get back from Wyoming.'

'Sure.'

'Robert won't see it – he'll have to be back at work by then. But, you know, we have to finish this now–'

'No problem.' He paused. 'Grace told me that you left your job. She said you weren't too unhappy about it.'

'No. I feel fine about it.'

'That's good.'

A silence fell between them. She looked over towards the fire and Tom followed her look. Robert was cooking.

'He's a good man, that husband of yours.'

'Yes, he is.'

'I was trying to decide who was luckier.' Annie looked at Tom. The sun was full on his face. He smiled. 'You, because you have him, or him, because he has you.'

They sat and ate, the children at one table and the adults at another. The sounds of talk and laughing filled the spaces between the trees, and the sun went slowly down.

After the meal, Grace asked Joe to show them all a trick with matches. He pushed two matches through his hair. Then he brought them together and they jumped into the air. Everyone laughed loudly. Robert watched closely, his eyes on Joe's fingers. He was a lawyer, so his job was to solve problems; he always needed to understand everything. Annie, sitting opposite him, wanted him to fail this time. She didn't want him to take away

Joe's fun.

'Oh, I see,' Robert shouted suddenly. 'Here, let me try.'

When he succeeded, he smiled. The other children shouted happily, but Joe was clearly not pleased.

'What about Tom's trick?' Grace called. 'Have you got that piece of rope?'

'Of course,' Annie said. She always kept it with her. It was the only piece of Tom she had. Without thinking, she took it out. Then she knew it was a mistake. She did not want Robert to understand the trick. This was between her and Tom; this was important.

Joe asked Robert to hold up his finger. Everyone was watching, except Tom. He was sitting back a little, watching Annie. He knew what she was thinking.

'Don't,' Annie said suddenly.

Everyone went quiet and looked at her.

'I . . . I just want to learn to do it for myself.'

Joe paused for a moment and looked at her. He saw that she meant it. He lifted the loop from Robert's finger and handed the rope back to Annie.

Her eyes met Robert's. She could see that he was hurt. Later, Tom saw her quietly putting the rope back into her pocket.

Chapter 10 Living for the Moment

Late on Sunday night, Tom did a final check on the horses. Then he went inside to pack.

'Get into bed, Scott,' Diane was shouting. 'We're catching a plane at seven in the morning and you need some sleep.'

Tom walked up the stairs and saw the half-filled cases.

'Come on, Scott,' said Tom, pushing him towards the bedroom. Craig was already asleep. Tom sat on Scott's bed and they talked about Disneyland until the boy's eyes closed.

Tom walked past Frank and Diane's room on the way to his own. She thanked him and said good night. Tom packed everything he needed for a week. It wasn't much. Then he tried to read, but he couldn't keep his mind on his book. He walked to the window and looked up towards the river house. Robert and Grace were on a plane for New York, and Annie was there, alone.

◆

Annie woke to the sound of a car. She knew that the Bookers were leaving for their flight. Was Tom there to say goodbye? She got out of bed and went to the window. She could see the car leaving. There was nobody outside the ranch house.

She had a bath and tried to choose some clothes. She tried one thing, then another. In the end she got angry with herself. She put on a pair of old trousers and a shirt. What did it matter? He was only coming to say goodbye.

Finally she saw him coming out of the house. He threw a bag in the back of his car and then walked up towards her.

'Hello.'

'Hello.'

'Did Grace and Robert get their flight all right?'

'Oh yes. Thanks. I heard Diane and Frank go.'

For a long moment there was silence.

'Would you like some coffee?'

'Oh. No thanks. I have to go.'

'OK.'

'Well.' He pulled a small piece of paper from his pocket. 'Here's my number in Wyoming. If there's a problem or something, you know.'

She took it. 'Thanks. When will you be back?'

'Oh. Saturday, I guess. One of the workers – Smoky – will be here tomorrow to look after the horses. I told him that you're feeding the dogs.'

She gave him a little smile.

'OK,' he said. She followed him to his car. He put his hat on.

'Well, goodbye Annie.'

'Goodbye.'

He started the car and touched his hat to her. Then he drove away.

◆

He drove for four and a half hours. And all the time the ache in his heart seemed to get worse. Why didn't he just take her in his arms? He knew that she wanted him to. And suddenly he understood. It was simple. He loved her deeply.

◆

It was for the best, Annie thought. She had all kinds of jobs to fill the day and the coming week usefully. But it wasn't so easy. The day was long, and she felt lonely.

She watched the sun going down behind the mountains. Then she drove down to feed the dogs. They happily led her to the place where their food was kept.

At that moment a car drove in and stopped in front of the ranch house. Annie was surprised that the dogs did not even turn their heads.

She saw him just before he saw her. For a long moment they didn't speak.

'I thought . . .' He stopped. 'I decided to come back.'

Annie looked into his eyes. 'Yes.'

She found that she couldn't move. He knew it and came to her. He put his arms around her and held her tightly.

And then she cried. He kissed the tears that ran down her face. She brought her lips to meet his.

'I can't believe you're here,' she said.

'I can't believe I went.'

He took her by the hand and led her into the ranch house. They climbed the wide stairs and walked slowly to his room.

He pulled her close to him and kissed her again.

Annie closed her eyes. There is nothing except this, she thought. No other time, no other place, than now and here. And there is no right or wrong. This is the way it has to be.

◆

He woke at first light and felt her warm body next to his. Her right hand lay on his chest just above his heart. He lay without moving, afraid to wake her. Then he heard the sound of a car. He got out of bed and quietly put on his clothes.

'Good morning, Smoky.'

'I thought you went to Wyoming.'

'Yeah. Change of plan. Sorry. I meant to call you.'

Smoky was looking at Annie's car now. 'Your guests didn't go back east then?'

'Well, Grace did, but her mother couldn't get a flight. She's staying here until Grace gets back.'

'Right,' Smoky said.

◆

Annie woke up and lay there for a moment. Then she remembered. But where was Tom? She ran to the window. There he was, talking to a young man.

There were two cups on the table when she came down to the kitchen a little later.

'I made some coffee.'

'Thanks.'

'That was Smoky. I forgot to call him.'

Silence. He looked so worried. She was suddenly afraid that he was going to say that it was all a mistake.

62

'Annie.'

'What?'

'I don't know what you feel about this . . .'

'And what do *you* feel?'

He said simply, 'That I love you.' Then he smiled in a way that almost broke her heart. 'That's all.'

She put her cup down and went to him. He held her close. She covered his face with kisses.

They had four days and three nights before the Bookers returned. Live for now, Annie told herself, with no thoughts of the past or the future. Then nothing afterwards mattered; this moment was theirs for ever.

Later, she told him what she wanted. They agreed to ride to the place where they first kissed. They planned to be alone together with the mountains and sky.

◆

Smoky saw Tom preparing the horses.

'Going up to check on the cattle?'

'Yes.'

'Alone or . . . ?'

'No, Annie's coming too.'

'Oh, right.'

'Smoky . . . I want to ask you something.'

'Sure.'

'Don't say anything about this, will you?'

'No, of course not. I understand.'

Before leaving, Tom went down to the fields. He put Pilgrim in with some of the younger horses. When Tom walked away, Pilgrim stood alone by the gate. He was watching Tom. He seemed to know that something in their lives was different now.

◆

They rode for some hours, speaking very little. It was enough to be together. There was no need for words.

They stopped in the heat of the afternoon and ate a simple meal. Later they climbed to the top of a hill. Suddenly Tom told Annie to stop. Not far in front of them they saw the group of wild horses. Tom counted seven full-grown females, two young horses and a large white stallion. He was deep-chested and strong.

'What a beautiful animal,' Annie said.

'Yes. Things get a bit difficult at this time of year,' said Tom. 'He'll have to fight other stallions who are following the females.'

The white stallion was looking at one of these males now. They stood nose to nose while the other horses looked on. Suddenly both animals seemed to go crazy. They lifted their front feet high and kicked angrily. Even from here you could see the whites of their teeth and eyes. Then, in moments, the fight was finished. The other stallion ran off. The white horse led his family away.

Tom and Annie talked for hours by the fire that night. He told her about Rachel and his son. She tried to describe her feelings for Robert.

'Did you want more children?'

'Oh, yes. We tried. But I was never able to carry them inside me for long. In the end we just gave up. More than anything, I wanted a child for Grace. A brother or a sister for her.'

They fell into silence again. Annie knew what he was thinking. But it was a thought that was too sad to talk about.

After two more happy days, the last night came. They had to return and be with the others again.

◆

Back at the house, Annie prepared their last meal together.

'Oh, Tom. I love you so much.'

Suddenly both animals seemed to go crazy.

'I love you too.'

When they finished eating, he asked her about the rope trick.

'Do you know how to do it yet?'

'No, I don't think so.'

'Did you keep the rope?'

'What do you think?'

She pulled it from her pocket and gave it to him. Then he very slowly showed her every move. Suddenly, she understood.

'Let me try,' she said. She found that she could picture exactly the movements of his hands. And it worked. When she pulled, the rope came free.

He sat back. She read both love and sadness in his face.

'Now you know,' he said.

'Can I keep the rope?'

'You don't need it now.' He took it and put it in his pocket.

Chapter 11   Love Hurts

Everyone was there, but Grace wanted to be alone. She looked at the waiting faces at the side of the arena: her mother, Frank and Diane, Joe, Scott and Craig, and even Smoky. She was afraid of failing.

Tom was in the middle, preparing Pilgrim. The horse looked beautiful. He seemed to sense that this was an important moment.

Tom rode him slowly around the arena a few times. Grace stood next to her mother. She tried to stay calm.

Then Tom got down from Pilgrim and walked over to Grace. She went to meet him. The new leg felt good.

'Ready?' he asked. He saw the worry in her face. When he got to her he said, very quietly, 'You know, Grace, we don't have to do this now. Not with all these people here.'

'It's OK. I don't mind.'

'Sure?'

'Sure.'

He put his arm around her shoulders and they walked over to Pilgrim. He lifted his ears when they came near.

Annie was nervous. This was such an important moment. But what was beginning and what was ending? Annie wasn't sure.

'She's a strong child, that daughter of yours,' Diane said.

'I know.'

Tom stopped Grace a little way away from Pilgrim and went the final few steps alone. He put his hand on Pilgrim's neck and his head close to the horse's. Pilgrim never took his eyes off Grace.

Even from her position on the outside, Annie knew that something was wrong.

When Tom tried to bring the animal to Grace, Pilgrim refused to move. He lifted his head and looked down at Grace. White showed at the top of his eyes. Tom turned him away and walked him round and round. This seemed to calm him. But when Tom led him back to Grace, he became frightened again.

Tom took Pilgrim away and walked him again. When that didn't work, he rode him a few times around the arena. But again the horse moved away when Tom took him towards Grace. This time he let Pilgrim go and took Grace to the side of the arena.

'OK Grace,' he said. 'We're going to try one more thing. I didn't want to do this. But there's something inside that horse that I can't reach in any other way. So I'm going to make him lie down. Smoky'll help me. OK?'

'OK,' said Grace. But she had no clear idea what this meant.

'What do you mean, exactly?' asked Annie.

'Well, it's more or less how it sounds. But I have to tell you that it's not always pretty to watch. Sometimes a horse will fight really hard. So if you prefer not to watch, please go inside. I'll call you when we're finished.'

'No,' replied Grace. 'I want to watch.'

Smoky went into the arena with ropes and talked to Tom. Pilgrim stood at the other side of the arena and watched.

Tom was near the animal now, and Smoky was a little way away. Pilgrim let Tom come near but kept his eyes on Smoky. Tom spoke quietly to the horse. He moved his hands down one of Pilgrim's front legs. Then he lifted the horse's foot and put a piece of strong cloth over it. A rope was tied to one end of the cloth. With this he lifted the weight of the foot off the ground and tied it in that position. Pilgrim was now a three-legged animal. He was not happy.

When Tom moved away, Pilgrim tried to move too. Then he discovered that he could not walk. He was angry too, and that made his fear worse. He jumped and moved his foot, trying to free it from the rope. Then he tried to run. Tom and Smoky held tightly to the ends of other ropes around his neck. Round and round he ran, like a crazy horse with a broken leg.

Tom looked over at Annie and Grace. Grace was pale and Annie had her arms around her.

'Why's he doing this?' Grace cried.

'I don't know.' It seemed so wrong to Annie. Tom was giving pain and suffering to this animal. She couldn't understand why.

Finally the horse stopped and the two men relaxed their ropes a little. Then he was moving again. Again they pulled their ropes tight until the animal had to stop. Pilgrim looked so tired and frightened. Annie wanted to shut her eyes. Tom tied his rope to a piece of wood at the side of the arena. He placed another rope around Pilgrim's neck and pulled down hard.

'What's he doing?' Grace's voice was small and frightened.

Frank said, 'He's trying to get him down on his knees.'

Pilgrim fought long and hard. Three times he went down and each time he got back up. But finally the horse crashed to its knees and stayed down.

But Tom didn't stop there. He shouted to Smoky and the two of them continued pulling on the ropes.

'Why don't they leave him alone?' Grace said. 'Isn't he hurting enough?'

'He's got to lie down,' Frank said.

Pilgrim was making terrible noises and again he fought for a long time. But it was all too much. He fell over on his side and lay his head on the sand.

Annie could hear Grace crying. Her own tears began to fall. Grace turned and lay her head on Annie's chest.

'Grace!' It was Tom. 'Will you come here, please?'

'No! I won't!'

He left Smoky and walked over to them. Annie kept her arms tightly around Grace.

'Grace? I'd like you to come with me.'

'No, I don't want to.'

'You've got to.'

'No, you'll only hurt him some more.'

'He's not hurt. He's OK.'

'Oh sure!'

Annie wanted to say something, to protect her daughter. But Tom's face was so hard, so frightening. She let him take her daughter by the hand. He turned to Grace and looked into her eyes.

'You've got to do this, Grace. Trust me.'

He led her across the arena. Annie followed behind, unable to leave her child at this moment.

'OK, Grace,' Tom said. 'I want you to touch him. I want you to start at the back, then do the legs. Feel him all over.'

'Why? He looks half dead.'

'Just do what I ask.'

Grace walked slowly around to the back of the horse. Pilgrim didn't lift his head. But he tried to follow her with his eyes.

'OK. Now touch him. Go on. Start with his leg there. Go on. Feel it.'

She put her hands on Pilgrim's back leg. The horse didn't move. She worked on his legs, then his body. Finally she touched his neck and head.

'OK. Now I want you to stand on him.'

'What!' Grace looked at him. 'Are you crazy?'

'Do what I say!'

Annie took a step towards them. 'Tom—'

'Be quiet, Annie.' He didn't even look at her. And now he almost shouted: 'Do what I say! Now!'

Grace started to cry. Tom took her hand and led her to the side of the horse.

'Now step up. Go on, step up on him.'

And she did. And with tears falling down her face, she stood there. A damaged person standing on the beaten body of the animal she loved most in all the world.

'Why are you doing this?' Annie cried. 'It's so terrible.'

'You're wrong,' he replied, helping Grace down. 'Pilgrim chose to do it.'

'What do you mean?'

Now he turned to look at her. Grace was crying at his side.

'He had to choose; to continue fighting life or to accept it.'

'You didn't let him choose.'

'Yes, I did. He chose to go to the edge of life and look over. He saw what was there. And he chose to come back. He chose to accept life.'

He turned to Grace and put his hands on her shoulders.

'Lying down like that was the worst thing that he could imagine. And you know what? He found it was OK. Even you standing on him was OK. The light only comes after the darkest hour. That was Pilgrim's darkest hour. And he's still here . . .

'Why are you doing this?' Annie cried. 'It's so terrible.'

he's still living. Do you understand?'

Grace was trying to understand. 'I don't know,' she said. 'I think so.'

'Annie? Do you understand? It's really important that you understand this. It's about what's in our hearts. About seeing clearly the way life is. Accepting it. It's about being true to it, never mind the pain. Because the pain of not being true to it is far, far greater. Annie, I know you understand this.'

She looked at him. She knew there was some message here, one that was only for her. It was not about Pilgrim, but about them. About everything that was between them. She didn't understand it then. Perhaps with time . . .

Grace watched them untie the ropes. Pilgrim lay there for a moment looking up at them with one eye. Then he slowly got to his feet and took a few steps.

Tom told Grace to lead him straight to the water at the side of the arena. She stood next to him while he took a long drink.

Then Tom joined them. He prepared the horse for riding and told Grace to get on. She put one foot up. Pilgrim didn't move. Tom took her weight and she lifted her leg over the horse's back.

She felt no fear. She walked him first one way around the arena and then the other. It was some time before she heard the others. They were laughing and shouting happily; it felt just like the day she rode Gonzo.

But this was Pilgrim. Her Pilgrim. He was better. And she could feel him under her, just like before, strong and trusting and true.

◆

The party was Frank's idea.

'We can't let Annie and Grace drive 2,000 miles home with that old horse without a party,' he said.

Tom dressed slowly in his room. He could hear cars arriving,

72

and voices and music. When he looked out, there was already a crowd. It was a fine, clear evening. He searched the faces and found her. She was wearing a new dress. She looked beautiful.

Diane got to Tom first.

'Can I have this dance?'

'I was just waiting for you to ask,' he replied.

'Smoky told me that you didn't go to Wyoming last week.'

'Well, that's right. I didn't.'

'Oh.'

'What is this, Diane?'

'You *know* what I'm talking about. It's a good thing she's going home.'

They didn't speak for the rest of the dance. When it ended, she gave him a knowing look. Then she went off. He was deep in thought when Annie came up behind him.

'Come and dance with me,' she said.

The music was fast. He wanted to hold her but he couldn't. The next one was a slow song. Finally they could touch. He held her close and could feel her body through her light dress. He knew that Diane was watching somewhere. But he wasn't worried.

'I need to talk to you,' Annie said in his ear.

'Outside. By the stables. I'll meet you. In 20 minutes.'

◆

Grace felt good. She danced with almost everyone. For the first time in her life she felt beautiful.

She went into the house, towards the downstairs bathroom, and she heard voices. Frank and Diane were having a fight.

'You've had too much to drink.'

'Be quiet,' she shouted.

'It's not your business, Diane.'

'She's wanted him from the moment she arrived.'

73

'Listen. He's a grown man.'

'And she's a married woman with a child.'

Grace stepped into the room.

'Hello,' she said lightly.

Frank and Diane turned quickly.

'Oh . . . hello, Grace. You having a good time?'

'I'm having a great time, thanks. Is it OK if I use the bathroom in here?'

'Of course it is. Go right in.'

She stood in the bathroom looking into the mirror. Who were they talking about? And then the thought came to her. No, it couldn't be.

◆

Annie arrived before him. Then, suddenly, he was there and she was holding him.

'I'm going to leave Robert,' she told him. 'I know the pain this will give to everyone. I know the damage that it will do. But I want to be with you. I love you.'

He listened in silence, holding her and running his fingers across her face.

'Oh Annie.'

'What? Tell me.'

'You can't do that.'

'I can. I'll go back to New York and tell him.'

'And Grace. You think you can tell Grace?'

She looked at him, searching his eyes. Why was he doing this?

'After what she has suffered . . . ?'

'You think I don't know?'

'Of course you do. And that's why you won't do this.'

She felt tears coming. She knew she couldn't stop them.

'I can't lose you. Don't you understand? Can *you* choose to lose *me*?'

'No,' he said simply. 'But I don't have to.'

'Remember what you said about Pilgrim? You said he went to the edge and looked over. And then he chose to accept life.'

'But if you see pain and suffering there? Then you're crazy to accept it.'

'But the pain and suffering will be other people's, not ours.'

He looked away. Annie was angry now.

'You don't want me.'

'Oh Annie. You'll never know how much I want you.'

She cried in his arms and lost all sense of time and place. When she could cry no more, he cleaned her face. Then they returned to the party.

Chapter 12   Saved

The next morning Annie felt terrible. She dressed. Then she went down to the kitchen to get some juice for Grace. There was so much to do. They had to pack and clean the house. They had to put oil and water in the car. They needed food for the journey…

She ran to the top of the stairs and called Grace's name. No answer. So she went into the bedroom. The bed was empty.

◆

Joe first discovered that Pilgrim was missing. They searched everywhere for him, calling his name. But they didn't find him.

'I'm sure it's OK. Grace has probably taken him for a ride,' said Diane.

Tom saw the fear in Annie's eyes. They both knew that it was something more.

'How was she when she went to bed?' Tom asked.

'Quiet. She said she felt a little sick. I think she was unhappy about something. Is Pilgrim safe enough for her to take out?'

'He'll be all right,' Tom replied. 'I'll go with Frank. We'll try and find her.'

The two of them went off to change their clothes.

'I think she knows,' Annie said quietly to Tom when he returned.

'Yes, I think so too.'

'I'm sorry.'

'Don't ever be sorry, Annie. Ever.'

◆

Grace rode Pilgrim fast, pushing him on and on. He did everything she asked. He ran and ran all morning. At first she was just angry; she had no plan. She only knew that she wanted to punish them. She wanted to make them sorry. But when she felt the cold air of the high places in her eyes, the tears came. She put her head on Pilgrim's and cried.

Why was Tom doing this? Her Tom. After all that kindness. This was what he was really like. Only a week earlier, he was talking and laughing with her father. A week! Adults were sick. And everyone knew about it. Everyone. It was all so sick.

A little later, Grace took Pilgrim to drink from a small river. While he was drinking, she found some matches in her pocket. That's when she had the idea.

She looked over the top of the hill towards a little wooden hut. At this time of year dry wood burnt like paper. And her body inside it. They were going to be sorry.

◆

Frank got down from his horse to take a closer look at the prints by the water's edge.

'I think she's going to the hut. From the look of these, she's about half an hour in front of us.'

The horses were drinking noisily when Frank said, 'Tom . . . it's not my business, but . . .'

'It's OK, Frank. Go on.'

'Well, you know Diane had a lot to drink last night . . .'

'Yes.'

'Well, we were in the kitchen and she was shouting about you and Annie . . .'

'Yes . . .'

'Then Grace came in . . . and I think she heard.'

'Oh.'

'Is that what this is about?'

'Yes, probably,' replied Tom.

'You're in it deep then?'

'Yes. You can say that.'

They looked for her from the top of the hill. But nothing. Frank got off his horse and looked at the ground. Not one horse's prints but many.

'I guess these are those wild Pryor Mountain horses.'

Then suddenly they heard it. There was a deep noise coming from somewhere in the trees. It was the sound of horses, running and screaming. Perhaps ten or more, Tom thought. He and Frank rode on slowly, listening all the time.

The narrow path that they were following went up. After some time the ground fell away and the path became wider. Many hundreds of feet below was a dark world of trees and rock. It was from this place that the sound of running horses came. They heard the scream of a single horse. And Tom knew, with a sick feeling, that it was Pilgrim.

◆

Grace had her back to a rock wall. All around her were horses, running and screaming. At the centre, hitting out with their feet,

77

were Pilgrim and the white stallion.

Tom got down from Rimrock. 'Stay here with the horses,' he told Frank.

He walked with his back to the wall. He never took his eyes off the horses.

He was very close to Grace now. Finally she saw him. Her face was very pale.

'Are you hurt?' he shouted.

Grace could not speak for fear – fear more for Pilgrim than herself. She could see the white stallion's strong teeth when they bit into Pilgrim's neck. Worst of all was the sound of the screams.

She saw Tom take off his hat and step out into the running horses. He held the hat high and moved it around in front of him. They turned away from him suddenly and he moved in quickly behind them. He pushed them before him, away from Pilgrim and the stallion. Soon the female horses and their young were gone.

Now Tom turned and moved slowly around the wall again. He stopped near Grace and called, 'Stay right there, Grace. You'll be OK.'

Then, without any sign of fear, he walked towards the fight. Grace saw his lips moving. She couldn't hear what he said. Perhaps he was talking to himself; perhaps he was not talking at all.

He didn't stop until he was next to them. Then they seemed to see him. He reached for Pilgrim's neck and pulled him down. He turned him and pushed him away from the stallion. This made the stallion even more angry. He turned towards Tom.

Grace never forgot what followed. It stayed with her until the day she died. The stallion turned, threw his head back and kicked at the ground with his feet. For a moment he did not know what to do with this man – this man who stood unafraid before him.

Tom did not move back; he walked closer to the stallion.

When he moved, the stallion lifted its legs. But Tom continued

78

to walk towards him. Grace thought that Tom opened his arms a little to the horse. And he seemed to show him his open hands. Perhaps he was offering what he always offered, the gift of trust. But Grace had a darker thought too. Tom seemed to be offering himself this time. Then, with a terrible sound, the stallion's feet came down on Tom's head. He fell like a stone to the ground.

The stallion brought his legs up again, but not so high. He threw his head high and screamed one last time. Then he was gone.

Chapter 13   A Year Later

Whose looks did the new baby have? It was too early to tell. His skin was fair and his hair was a light brown. And his eyes were sky blue from the day of his birth three months before.

Tom Booker lay next to his father now. Annie knew this from Frank. His letter arrived on a Wednesday morning in late July when she was alone. She already knew then that she was carrying a child.

Frank also wrote about a conversation that Tom had with Joe before he died. He wanted to give Grace a present: Bronty's baby. So Frank was sending the young horse east with Pilgrim.

Both horses lifted their heads when Annie walked into the field. Then they calmly continued eating the grass. Grace worked with the young horse, now almost a year old, every weekend. She never pushed the young animal too hard. Just helped him to help himself. He was doing well. Grace named him Gully.

Annie couldn't remember much about the week that followed Tom's death. And it was probably best that way. They left when Grace was fit to travel. They flew back to New York. For days the girl did and said almost nothing.

But when the horses arrived that August morning, Grace

But Tom continued to walk towards him.

changed. They seemed to unlock a door inside her, and for two weeks she cried. And then all the pain was out. She seemed to decide, like Pilgrim, that she wanted to live. She became an adult.

In the autumn she went back to school. The welcome that she received there from her friends helped a lot. And when Annie finally told her about the baby, she showed only happiness. She never once asked who the father was.

Robert, too, did not ask. He wanted to believe that this was, perhaps, his child. That, at least, was Annie's feeling. She told him everything after they returned from Montana. But they did not want to decide about their future together. Not then. Grace was more important. So Annie stayed in Chatham and Robert in New York. Grace went from one to the other.

At first, Robert dropped Grace at her mother's and then left. Few words passed between them. Then, one night in October, Grace asked him to stay. He slept in the guest room and went the next morning. After that, he spent one night in the guest room each weekend. His leaving time the next day got later and later.

The baby was born in early March. Robert and Grace were there for the birth. They all cried and laughed together. They called him Matthew, after Annie's father.

Annie heard the baby crying. She fed him. Then she took him into the house and changed him. He watched her with those clear blue eyes while she prepared supper. Perhaps she should ask Robert to stay all weekend this time.

◆

There was one other thing that Frank sent with his letter last summer. It was an envelope with Annie's name on it, from the table in Tom's room.

Annie looked at the envelope for a long time before she opened it. Inside, in a sheet of plain white paper, was the loop of rope. On the paper were the words 'Never forget'.

ACTIVITIES

Chapters 1–3

Before you read

1 Chapter 1 of the book is called *The Accident*. Is riding dangerous, do you think? How do people on horses have accidents?

2 Find these words in your dictionary. Use them in the sentences below.

clinic horn needle ranch rope

a Use a .... to tie that horse to the gate.

b A .... is part of a hospital.

c The car .... makes a loud noise when you press it.

d In America, a very big farm where sheep, cows or horses are kept is called a ....

e The doctor uses a .... to put medicine under your skin.

3 Find these words in your dictionary.

stable trailer truck trust

Which word means:

a a box on wheels that is pulled behind a car?

b the feeling that someone is honest and good?

c a big vehicle that carries large amounts of things?

d a building for horses?

After you read

4 Match the names and the sentences.

Grace   Judith   Gulliver   Pilgrim   Logan
Robert   Annie   Mrs Dyer   Tom Booker

a This is the name of Grace's horse.

b Annie is her mother.

c Grace is his daughter.

d She is Grace's friend.

e Grace's friend is riding this horse.

f She has an important job at a magazine.

g She owns some stables.

h He is a horse doctor.

i He helps horses who have problems with their riders.

5 What is the result of the accident for:

    a Grace?   **b** Judith?   **c** Pilgrim?   **d** Gulliver?

6 Work in pairs.

    Student A: You are the truck driver. Describe
                    the accident to Logan.

    Student B: You are Logan. Listen and ask questions.

7 Explain why Annie telephones Tom.

Chapters 4–6

Before you read

8 Tom Booker has refused to help Pilgrim. What do you think Annie is going to do now?

9 Find these words in your dictionary and answer the questions.

    arena brand cattle

    a Is an *arena* an *open* or *closed* area?

    b Is a *brand burned* or *painted* onto an animal?

    c Is *cattle* the word for a lot of *cows* or a lot of *sheep*?

After you read

10 Who is speaking? Who are they talking to? What is the situation?

    a 'How long is this going to continue? . . . Is this the way that you and I are going to be now?'

    b 'Excuse me for saying it . . . But you can't accept no for an answer, can you?'

    c 'I don't want to know anything about this, OK? It was all her idea. I think it's crazy. They should just let him die.'

    d 'There . . . look at that . . . that's a perfect brand. The best of the day.'

    e 'While you're working on that horse of theirs, Annie and Grace could live in the river house.'

    f 'I've got all these young horses to ride and poor old Rimrock here is not getting enough exercise. Would you ride him?'

    g 'She looked so little, so afraid. And I didn't save her. I let her die!'

11 What does Tom think that Pilgrim's problem is?

12 How do you think these people feel about each other? Give reasons for your opinions.

a Annie and Tom
b Annie and Grace
c Grace and Tom

Chapters 7–9

Before you read
13 What do we know about Annie now?
14 Find these words in your dictionary and use them in the sentence below.
loop   trick
Tom does a ^{1}.......... with a ^{2}.......... of rope.

After you read
15 Are these sentences true or false? Correct the false ones.
   a Annie is a very hard and cold person in her job.
   b Grace succeeds in riding Gonzo.
   c Grace tells her mother about riding Gonzo.
   d Everything is going well with Annie's job.
   e Annie can do the rope trick.
   f Annie and Tom are falling in love.
   g Tom does not like Robert.
   h Grace breaks her false leg.
16 Explain how Robert, Annie and Tom feel about the rope trick. Then work in groups of four. Act out the last part of Chapter 9. Take the parts of Joe, Robert, Annie and Tom.

Chapters 10–12

Before you read
17 How do you think the story will end for:
   a Grace?   **b** Annie?   **c** Robert?   **d** Pilgrim?
18 Find these words in your dictionary. Match each word with its opposite.
   edge   stallion
   1 edge   **a** a female horse
   2 stallion   **b** centre

After you read

19 Complete these sentences.
   a Robert and Grace go to . . .
   b Frank, Diane and the children go to . . .
   c Tom drives for four and a half hours. Then he decides to . . .
   d Tom takes the rope away from Annie because . . .
   e Tom has prepared Pilgrim for Grace to ride. Grace cries because . . .
   f Grace runs away with Pilgrim because . . .
   g She plans to . . .
   h When Tom and Frank find Grace, Pilgrim is fighting with . . .
   i Tom saves Grace and Pilgrim but . . .
20 Explain how Tom prepares Pilgrim for Grace to ride.
21 Describe how Tom saves Pilgrim.

Chapter 13

Before you read

22 The last chapter is called *A Year Later*. What do you think these people are doing?
   a Robert   **b** Annie   **c** Grace

After you read

23 Who is Matthew's father, do you think? Why do you think that?
24 Did Tom know that he was going to die? Give reasons for your opinion.
25 What do you think the future holds for Annie and Robert?

Writing

26 Write a short report for a newspaper. Describe the accident at the beginning of the story.
27 Write about Tom's short life for a horse-lovers' magazine.
28 How do Tom's feelings for Annie and Annie's feelings for Tom change during the story?
29 Explain the importance of the rope trick to the story.

30 You are Grace. It is one year after Tom's death. Write a letter to Frank.Tell him what you are doing. Tell him about your feelings for Tom.

31 A friend is thinking of reading the book. Write about the story. Say what you think about it.

1 Yes, because the horse can be extiting and you can fall.

2 a vape
b clinic
c horn
d ranch
e needle

3 a trailer
b trust
c truck
d stable

4 a Pilgrim
b Grace
c Robert
d Judith
e Gulliver
f Annie
g Mrs Dyer
h Logan
I Tom booker

5 a She have just one leg.
b She is dead.
c He is hurt.
d He is dead.

6

7 Because, He work at the Clinic For nervous horses. To help Pillgrim.

8 She will call him again. She will convince him

9 a close
b burned
c cows

10 a The mother to Grace
b Tom to annie
c Grace to Tom
d Tom to Grace
e Frank to Tom
f Tom to Annie
g Grace to Tom

11 Pilgrim is too sick and crazy

12 Annie love Tom

13 Angry, misunder

14 Friendly He goes crazy.

15 She makes all the decisions.

~~16~~ a trick
    b loop
~~16~~ a True
    b True
    c false
    d false
    e True
    f True
    g True

17. She sucsite to riding pillgrim

she will mari robert

He will be nice.